AGE IS JUST A NUMBER: A NOTABLE GUIDE ON FINDING LOVE IN OLD AGE

Bryan Wayne

Table of content

Why Does It Take Longer To Find Love As You Grow Older?

There are several reasons why more individuals are living alone. But, for others, living solitary is not a result of choice, but rather, one grown from the circumstance. Some of us would want to live with a spouse but find finding love difficult as we get older. But why?

Accepting yourself and accumulating life experience

As we become older, we unavoidably gather life experiences. Part of this is learning to accept ourselves as we are. Many talks of attaining a degree of self-confidence and self-love we wish we had in our childhood. In terms of finding a spouse, this is tremendously positive: we cannot begin to share love effectively with another person until we have a love for ourselves. But it also means it might take longer for us to locate a mate. When learning to love and cherish ourselves, we also know we deserve a spouse who values and loves us just as much. When discovering our value, we expect a spouse to live up to it.

A possible spouse has more things to complete - we're growing fussier

While this shouldn't make it impossible to locate someone, it may extend the process since we have a few more 'boxes to tick'. It may be stated that once older, we've possibly lost the romantic naïveté of our youth. It's no longer enough to be physically attracted to someone or to love their personality; there are a lot more practical concerns at play after you've got a little more life experience.

We are maybe too eager to discard prospective partners

As so, we might become guilty of "treating dating like a job interview". If a date does not check all of your boxes and passes the initial meeting or preliminary interview, the possible partner is not judged qualified for a second date.

Some might say there is no time to spend on individuals who you know from the onset are not appropriate for you. But, the trouble with this is, the older we grow, the more boxes we add to our list. This is sensible since we learn to know ourselves better, and therefore come to grasp more clearly what we'd want in a relationship too.

However, it is easy to fall into the trap of adding too many boxes that don't truly matter as much. It's as if we forget two individuals might be romantically compatible without having the same values and interests. It might be tempting to write someone off after one encounter if they do not fit all of our standards, but getting to know someone takes time. Perhaps readjusting priorities and maintaining an open mind, mean at least creating a nice buddy can be made.

Our lives are bigger and busier with little time for finding a mate

In the same manner, as we get older, our lives may become richer. Busy with a job, a busy social life, a pastime you like, traveling, spending time with children from a previous relationship, or visiting other family members. With so much going on, it might be hard to find time to meet new people or get back into dating. Again, readjusting priorities could assist here –

or rearranging how you spend your time to be more open to meeting someone new.

We appreciate our own space

A simple reason for the growing trend of living alone is that more of us desire and are blissfully enjoying our own space. Again, to love your own company is a beautiful thing, but it may make us apprehensive about going into a relationship. We may worry about sharing our space with someone. Although he has a girlfriend, TV Presenter Alex Zane has lived alone for six years, since it is his desire. He can establish a balance between his isolation and his connection that is like "a well-oiled machine".

This is not unusual - there are many people out there who love their isolation as much as Zane does, but he is live evidence that it need not hamper your dating prospects. In one of our posts, Elena tells about how living apart together works for her and her spouse. They are in a serious relationship yet have decided not to live together.

We search for more meaningful and fulfilling partnerships

Finally, the older we become, the more profound a connection we crave. As we age we become a lot more self-reliant, self-assured, and self-loving and less likely to require a partnership in our life to feel secure or valued.

We desire more than simply companionship in our relationship; we seek for it to be gratifying and meaningful. Therefore, while it could appear as if it takes longer to find a mate than it did when we were young, in actuality, this may be because we are more knowledgeable of what makes for a meaningful and enduring relationship.

The changing status of women

This is maybe even more essential for women seeking partnerships. A major societal development leading to the increase of more women living alone is the women's rights movement. Women acquiring equal chances to males have meant marriage is no longer a financial necessity; we can pay for ourselves, and even live alone if we wish. This may explain why some women may believe it has grown tougher to find a mate: now that having a partner is no longer a pre-requisite for a good existence, we emphasize seeking a relationship that is more meaningful and emotionally gratifying.

We are more comfortable with ourselves and living alone

We're realising life solitary can be pleasant and satisfying without a companion. Whatever the reasons, it is crucial to remember that the most important connection we have in life is the one we have with ourselves. Being able to concentrate on important 'me time and developing our distinct interests and hobbies is a benefit of living solitary and something which makes finding a mate more complicated. We might be challenged by the benefits being alone can provide, while at the same time weighing up the desire and realities of integrating a new person into our life.

For many of us, living alone is a long-term goal and a delightful way of life too. Some studies even show that living alone might contribute to higher happiness since it drives us to mingle more beyond our homes and close relatives. We're able to spend time fostering connections on our terms. While some may have found themselves stuck in miserable relationships by the rigorous limitations of cultural expectations, we are blessed to experience contentment in our own company and live more comfortably and effortlessly without the presence of a spouse.

It's not unreasonable to state, living arrangements and the way we conduct our relationships are growing more diversified - breaking previously traditional and accepted conventions. As we come to enjoy the benefits of living alone, and becoming more accepting of who we are and what we want, it means looking for a partner can inevitably take more time.

If you're a single man or woman over 50 entering the world of mature dating, there's a good chance you haven't dated since you were in your twenties. Don't worry. Finding true love can happen to anyone, at any age.

Here are seven ways that finding love in old age is better than it ever could be as a youngster. It could be enough to make a single millennial wish they were a boomer.

1 – Mature dating is more authentic.
To find real, authentic love, you first must know and love yourself well. As we reach 50 and beyond, most of us can say we've learned a lot about ourselves along the way. Life changes us and it's easier to be exactly who we're supposed to be.

While we were dating in our twenties, we dealt with the awkwardness of a growing body, mind, and spirit. Nothing, it seemed, was easy or graceful.

During those formative years, we defined ourselves by fitting into how we believed others thought we should be. We looked outside ourselves for acceptance and definition.

Happily, life is a good teacher. If we're open to it, we've learned to strip away the masks and simply be ourselves. That makes finding love in old age so much easier.
However, along the way, you might have been through a divorce or lost your partner to death. Major events like this can make it hard to escape the roles you played for many years. You cling to them for comfort in a time of change.

Finding a true, loving partner requires that you present yourself accurately to others. It's essential to strip away that which doesn't reflect who you truly are or worse, that which buries your true personality.

Depending on your previous relationships, you might be comfortable with co-dependent behaviors that mask your authentic self which in turn, sabotages your future relationships. If so, you must learn how to love yourself again.

This is best done with the aid of a professional counselor or therapist. Such introspective work pays dividends far above the effort involved. It's the only way to attract the right person for you.

2 – We're more experienced now.
If we're dating after fifty or sixty, we've likely had one or more partnerships or marriages. Sometimes we're hopeful of finding true love after divorce. This means that by now, we should have a pretty good idea of what we want and don't want in our potential partner.

If we were clever about our growth when we were younger, we learned how to handle relationship challenges to be better spouses. We don't have to bumble through the learning curve again.

Although we never stop learning since life never stops teaching, as mature daters, we get to depend on all those years of experience. We're typically comfortable in all types of scenarios which means we can easily meet and date new individuals.

3 – It's simpler, to be honest with people and ourselves today.
We don't worry so much about what others think of us. We're comfortable with who we are and that makes it simple, to be honest. We're not scared to be who we are because we have trust that somewhere, some way, we'll be linked with our perfect spouse.

When we're honest, it makes us more desirable to our fellow older daters. An article on Hello! alludes to a Saga Dating poll in which

"...76 percent of people in the senior group [50+] say certain qualities such as appearance and money become less relevant when seeking a new companion. And although both generations perceive a strong sense of humor to be crucial, the over 50s put a higher value on honesty with eight in ten searching for this in a mate compared to only 66 percent of twenty-somethings."

4 – We have more of a feeling of freedom.
When I first contemplated online dating, I had already determined that if I were unmarried for

the rest of my life, I'd still be perfectly content. Sure, I thought it would be lovely to find a lady with whom to enjoy those years, but I was OK if I didn't. I wasn't tied to the result.

It took me years to learn to detach from anticipated results, but it provided me with a calm feeling of freedom I never experienced while young. The reality is that I will lose the things I have, and I won't receive all the things I desire.

But I've also learned that the unexpected consequences frequently transcend anything that I could have envisioned. One of those unexpected results emerged in the shape of my true love and companion, Daisy.

5 – It's more enjoyable to date later in life.
All of the features I listed above make adult dating more pleasurable.

Society (for the most part) embraces a broad variety of partnerships that span ethnic, racial, age, and religious divides.

Women and men over 60 have lots of tales to tell and share that we didn't have as kids. Stories are wonderful to tell, whether it's on a first date or with your new-found relationship.

When we go on a fun date in which there's probably no potential for a relationship, we don't regard it as a failure. It's enjoyable. We get to meet a new individual and witness a distinct viewpoint on life and the world. There's a richness in meeting new people and having fun with them. Healthy fun can be an end unto itself.

6 – Older women and men are more emotionally mature.
Maybe you could sum all this up in one word—maturity. We are, after all, talking about adult dating. But life is tough, to sum up, or categorize so succinctly.

At this point in our lives, every one of us can say we've been through a few emotional wringers. If we learned nothing else, we learned to not allow our emotions to govern our conduct and choices as we did when we were young. After all, emotions are strong yet ephemeral. In adulthood, we have the awareness to halt and consider feelings before acting. It makes for a calm existence. It makes you a better date and a possibly better ideal companion.

How to find love in old age and keep it

Things you should know

Know What You Want: When you were younger, you probably dated for the fun of the experience. But as you age you realize that you become picky with who you date. Do you want a relationship? Or do you just want to have a good time after a bad divorce? Being clear on your motives for dating helps you choose a better-suited partner.

Be Honest About What You Want: Being honest with your partner lets them know where you stand. You aren't making promises you cannot keep. It keeps both of you on the same page.

Take Your Time: You don't have to deep dive into all the aspects of dating right away. Take your time to sort through them slowly. Look at it as an opportunity to rediscover what you like about dating.

Take Time To Heal: Maybe you're reeling from the loss of your partner or a nasty divorce experience. It is important to take your time to heal. A rebound relationship might be a great idea when you're in your 30s, but after your 60s you might find yourself looking for something else. If you don't take time to heal, that experience might not go as well as you hoped.

Be Open To A New Experience: You have to be ready to go out there and be open to experiencing new things. It doesn't mean you have to instantly download a dating app. But you may be open to meeting someone at your grocer, church, or a local singles meet. Be open to communicating about yourself and getting to know the other person. Be open to also letting them know when you aren't comfortable with anything. Your first date after your 60s may not go so well, but be open to viewing it as a learning experience.

Boost Yourself: Dating beyond your 60s could be intimidating, especially since you don't appear as you did in your 20s. Your confidence may also have taken a knock. It is time for you to remind yourself how magnificent you are. Look back on your life's journey and recollect all the events that made you, you! Don't be hesitant to gaze into the mirror before a date and give yourself a confidence-boosting pep talk.

Online Dating: After your 60s, you may not want to join a dating app or website and meet someone online. But it is a terrific method to meet new individuals. If this is something you are open to attempting, be sure you go about it safely. Don't give personal information to someone unless you have met them and can be assured of who they are. You must take safeguards before meeting someone physically whom you have known online. Meet them in a restaurant, and have a simple way to depart if you notice something dodgy. Don't invite them home or get into a vehicle with them on the first encounter. Make sure your family and friends know that you're out with this individual. And most importantly, watch out for fraudsters.

Health Checks: Being older makes you more prone to sickness. Make sure you are on top of your health. Also, make sure your spouse is on top of their health. This is extremely important when you get physical with someone.

Sometimes, when you get back out there, you might make a few mistakes. Here are a few common mistakes that can be avoided.

Think of age as simply a number: Finding an acceptable match frequently has more to do with emotional and physiological age than a person's numerical age, in and of itself. You want to be able to share comparable experiences and ideals if you're seeking a deeper form of love. Matching with someone's energy and activity level may also make for a more durable connection.

If you're 50, you may discover a terrific match with someone who's 38 or 62. Be open on both sides of the age spectrum.

Some men may want to date someone 10 or 20 years younger than them. Think about whether that partner's maturity matches your own. If you're active, there are many ladies in their 50s and beyond who may be a terrific fit.

Some women may feel like they are competing with younger, more youthful appearing ladies.

Think about how both sexes are frequently drawn to confidence more than anything else. Be confident in your skin.

Try speed dating: Search online for speed dating events, and discuss with a single buddy who may be willing to attend with you. This might be a fast method to meet new individuals, and see if there is an initial spark.
When speed dating, it's a quick interaction with a bigger number of potential individuals, therefore there's the advantage of not spending as much time, compared to getting set up by friends or seeing people one at a time via internet dates.
[8]
Think of it as a networking gathering, or a cocktail party. It's a short and quick method to meet people.

Consider joining a singles group: With current technology, there are dozens of methods to locate events for singles in your town. Here are some more sites that could offer single's groups:

A local church, or other houses of worship, that provides singles' activities.
Fitness organizations or clubs, such as a runner's group
General interest groups, such as via Meetup.com
Networking or college alumni gatherings
Volunteer groups
Social dance lessons

Consider how things may have changed: If you're just starting back into dating following a divorce or loss of a spouse, it may have been a while since you last went on a date. Tune into current dating conventions by questioning buddies who have been dating. Be open to sharing the cost with your date, meeting at a place instead of being picked up, maybe dating more than one person at a time, etc. Another wonderful approach to discovering contemporary dating norms? Just hop straight into it!

Show your enthusiasm for love and life: Being optimistic and enthusiastic about life is an appealing attribute. While you may feel burnt by love in the past, attempt to set aside previous sentiments. If you feel like you still aren't "over" a prior relationship, you may be carrying baggage that makes you less appealing to others. Consider the following:

Avoid making your prior relationships become the major focus of discussion when first meeting someone.

Talk about the things that make you sincerely joyful. Share tales that make you grin each time you tell them.

Find strategies to stay optimistic about love and dating truly and honestly. Seek assistance, or even therapy, if you keep coming into difficulties concerning how to move over your ex or past toxic relationships.

Common Mistakes Made By Men And Women Dating

Trying To Fit In: Getting back into the dating groove might be tricky, but don't try to do what the younger population is doing. When you're dating, find out what works best for you and do that. Forcing oneself to enjoy something could only damage your experience.

Taking It Too Seriously: A relationship is incredibly serious, but when you're just getting back out into the dating world you may want to take a pause and simply go for a test drive. It is totally good to not make things serious. You may have fun with dating, and it does not have to be serious.

Dating An Ex: Because it has been so long since you dated, you could believe it is a good idea to date an old flame. While it may work, remember that there was a reason you both separated in the first place. It is tempting to get caught up in feelings with an ex, so take your time and go gently. Dating an ex could be enjoyable, but it can also be like opening a can of worms.

Not Taking Your Health Seriously: Just because you are older doesn't mean you shouldn't know all your choices health-wise. Visit a doctor and chat with them about what you need to be aware of before you become physically connected with someone.

Dating After A Divorce: It is tempting to allow the emotions of a prior relationship to flow over into a new one. Give yourself time to move on from the divorce and your ex, feel comfortable with the thought of trusting someone new, and then start dating again. Don't leap into a relationship or make your new partner liable for your ex's faults.

Dating After A Loss: Many people will suggest it is time to move on and get back out there. But you must take your time to recuperate. You have lost someone who was highly significant and dear to you.

www.ingramcontent.com/pod-product-compliance
Lightning Source LLC
La Vergne TN
LVHW020544160826
845677LV00015B/4202
* 9 7 9 8 3 5 4 8 8 2 3 5 9 *